OPHTHALMOLOGY

for kids

First paperback edition March 2022

Book design by Betty Nguyen & Brandon Pham

ISBN 978-1-957557-01-4 (paperback)

Printed in the United States of America

Published by Black Phoenix Press

www.mdforkids.org

To the friends and family who have supported and loved us unconditionally, and to the mentors who have guided and taught us more that we could have imagined:

Thank you.

Betty & Brandon

Ophthalmology

(off-thuhl-MAA-luh-jee)

the branch of medicine concerned with the study and treatment of disorders and diseases of the eye

The **eye** is an organ that lets us see the world.

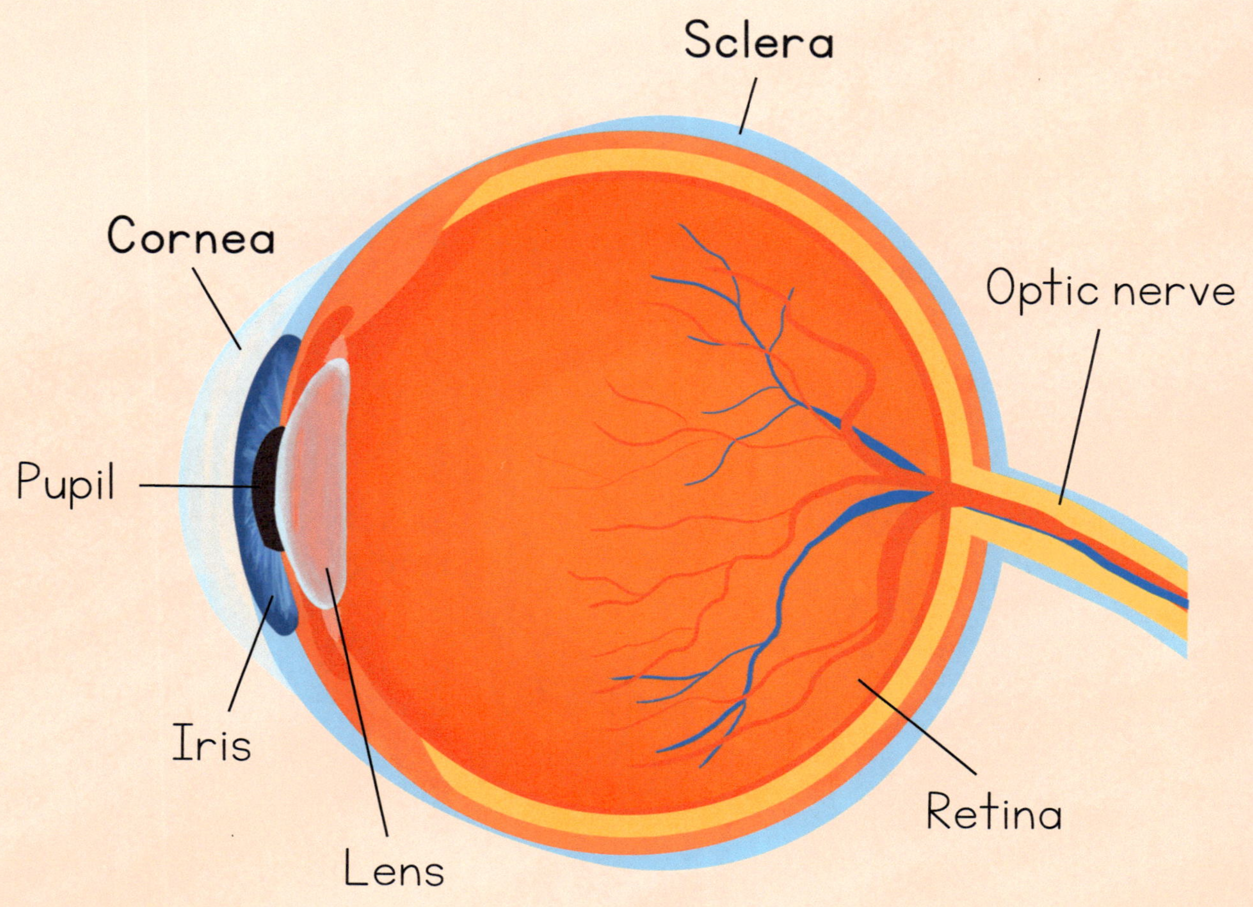

The outer part of the eye is made up of the **cornea** and **sclera**, which both protect the eye.

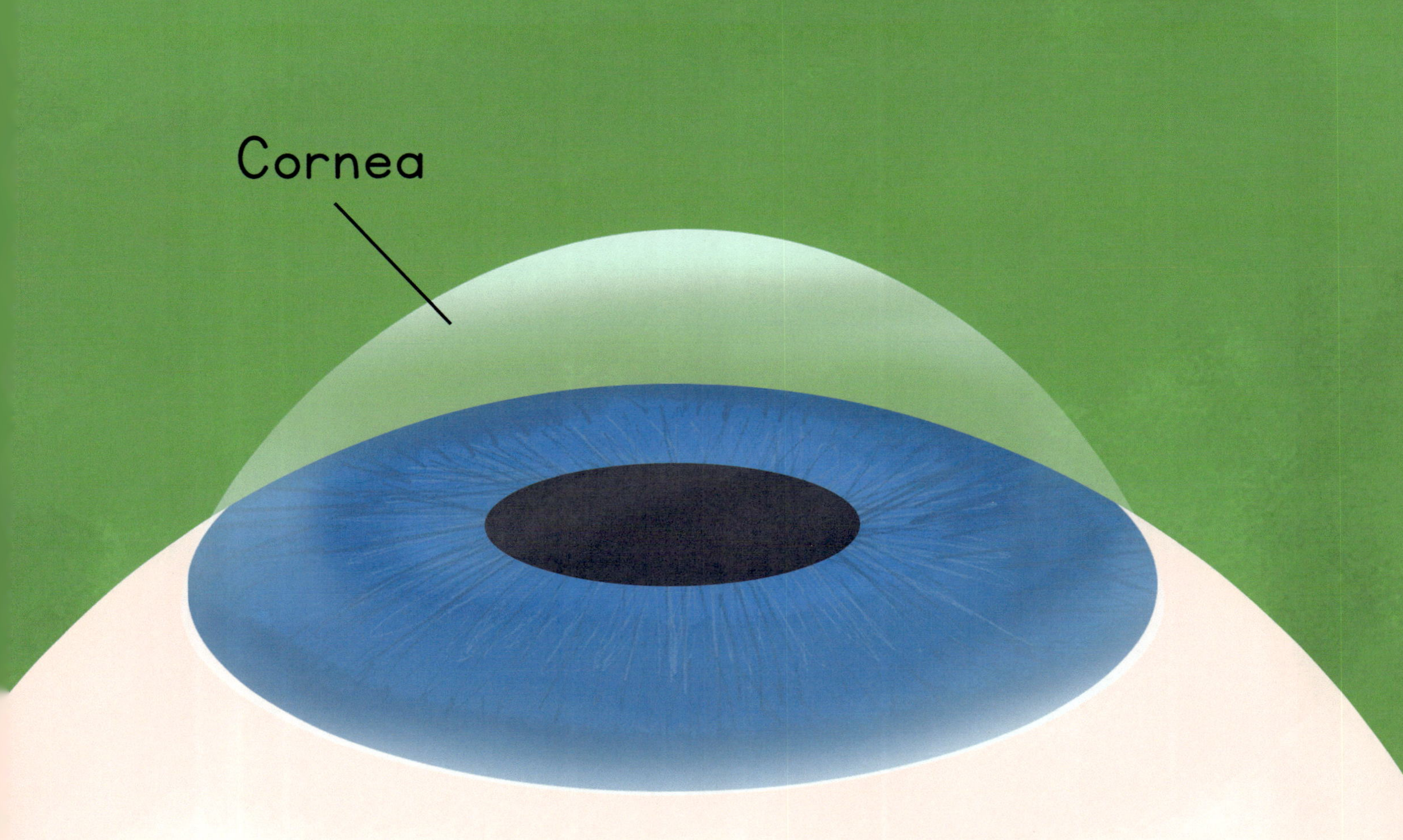

The **cornea** is the front clear layer of the eye that helps focus light onto the back of the eye.

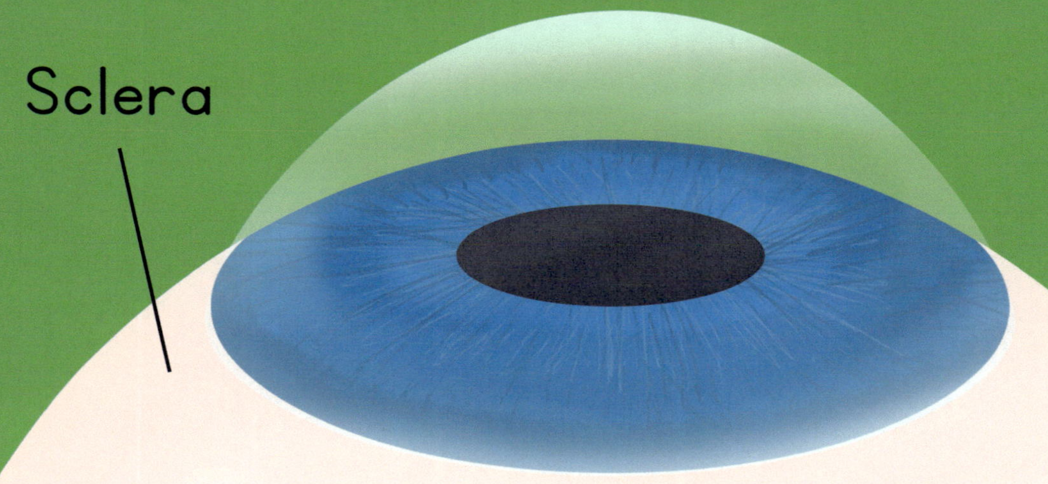

The **sclera** is the outer white layer that covers the rest of the eye.

Behind the cornea is the **iris**, which is the colored part of the eye.

Irises can be many different colors, such as brown, hazel, blue, gray, and amber. What color are *your* irises?

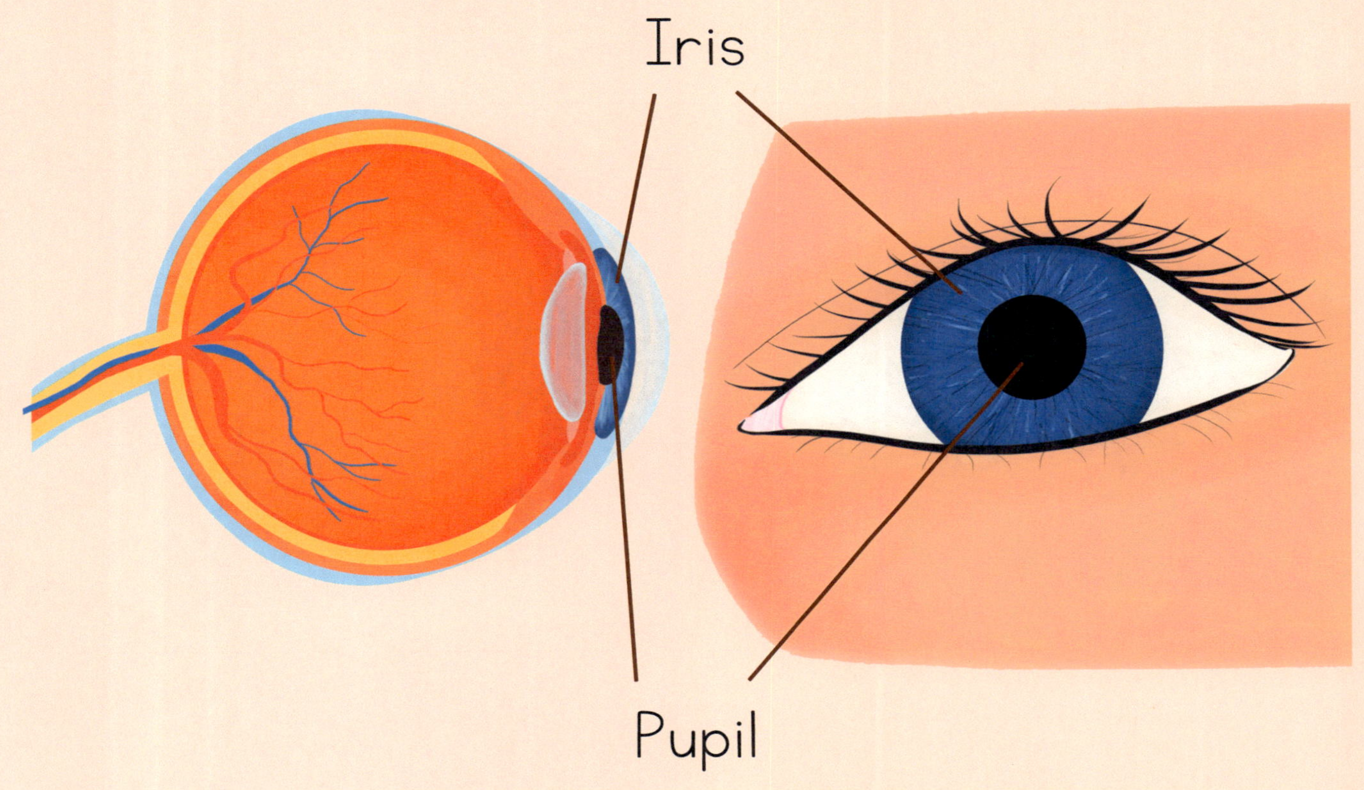

In the center of the iris is a small opening called the **pupil**, which allows light to enter the eye.

Bright light

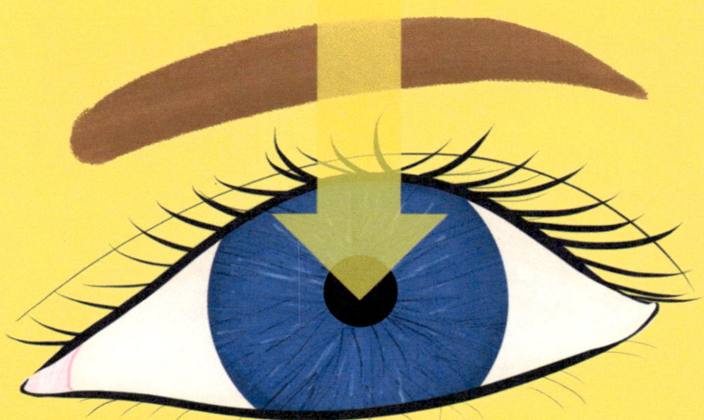

Dim light

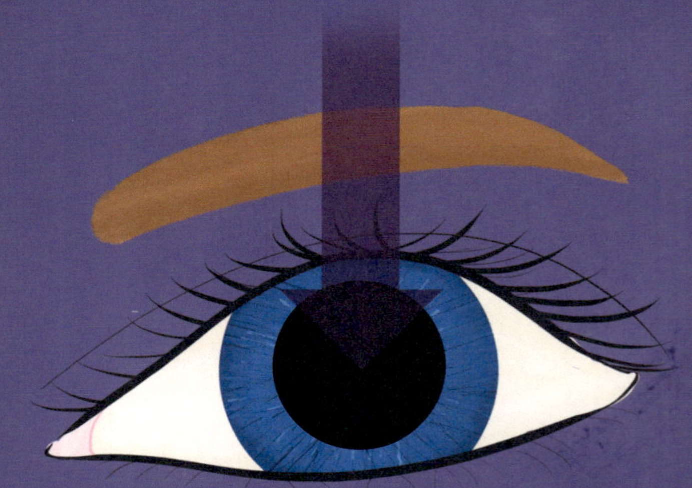

The iris controls the size of the pupil.
In *bright light*, the pupil becomes *smaller*.
In *dim light*, the pupil becomes *larger*.

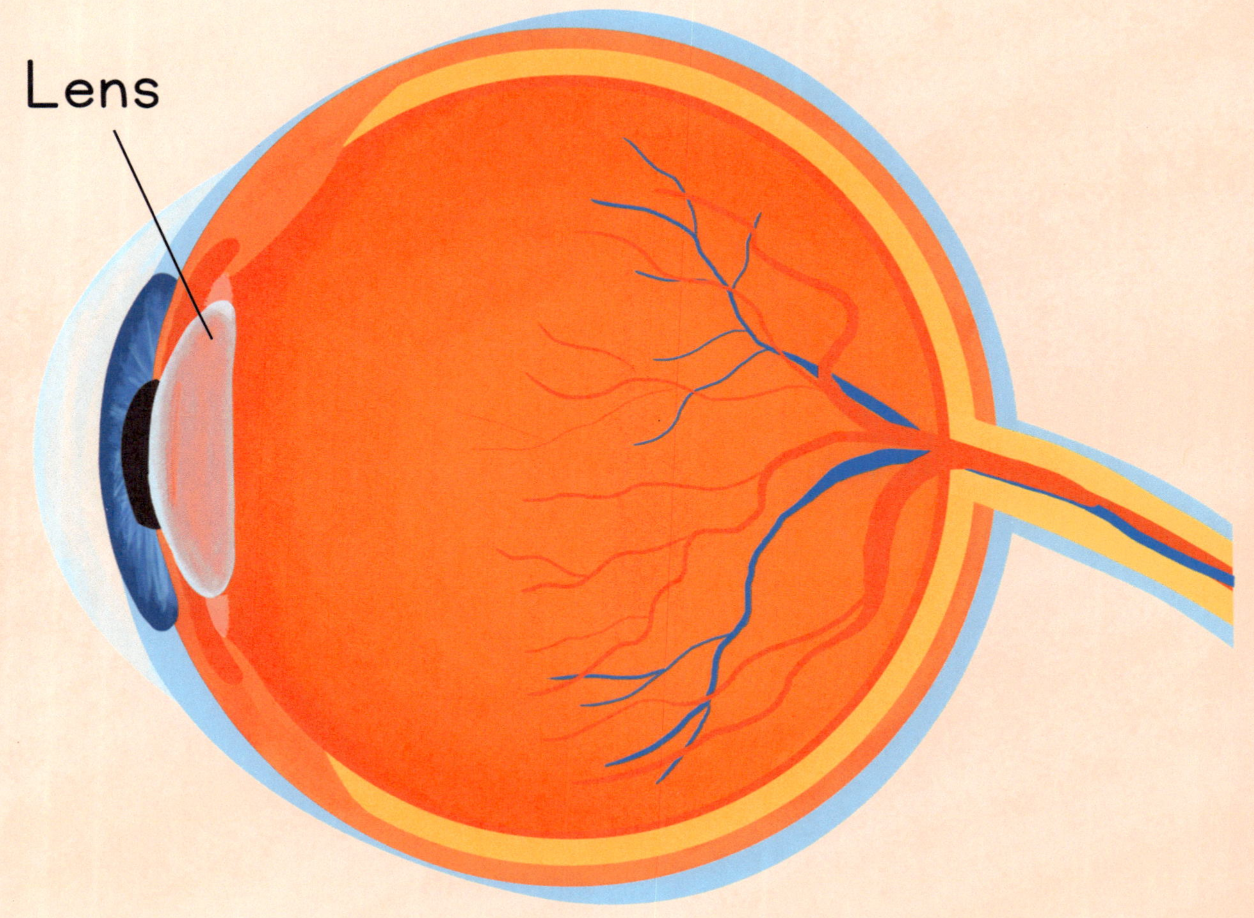

Behind the iris is the **lens,** which is clear and helps focus light onto the back of our eye.

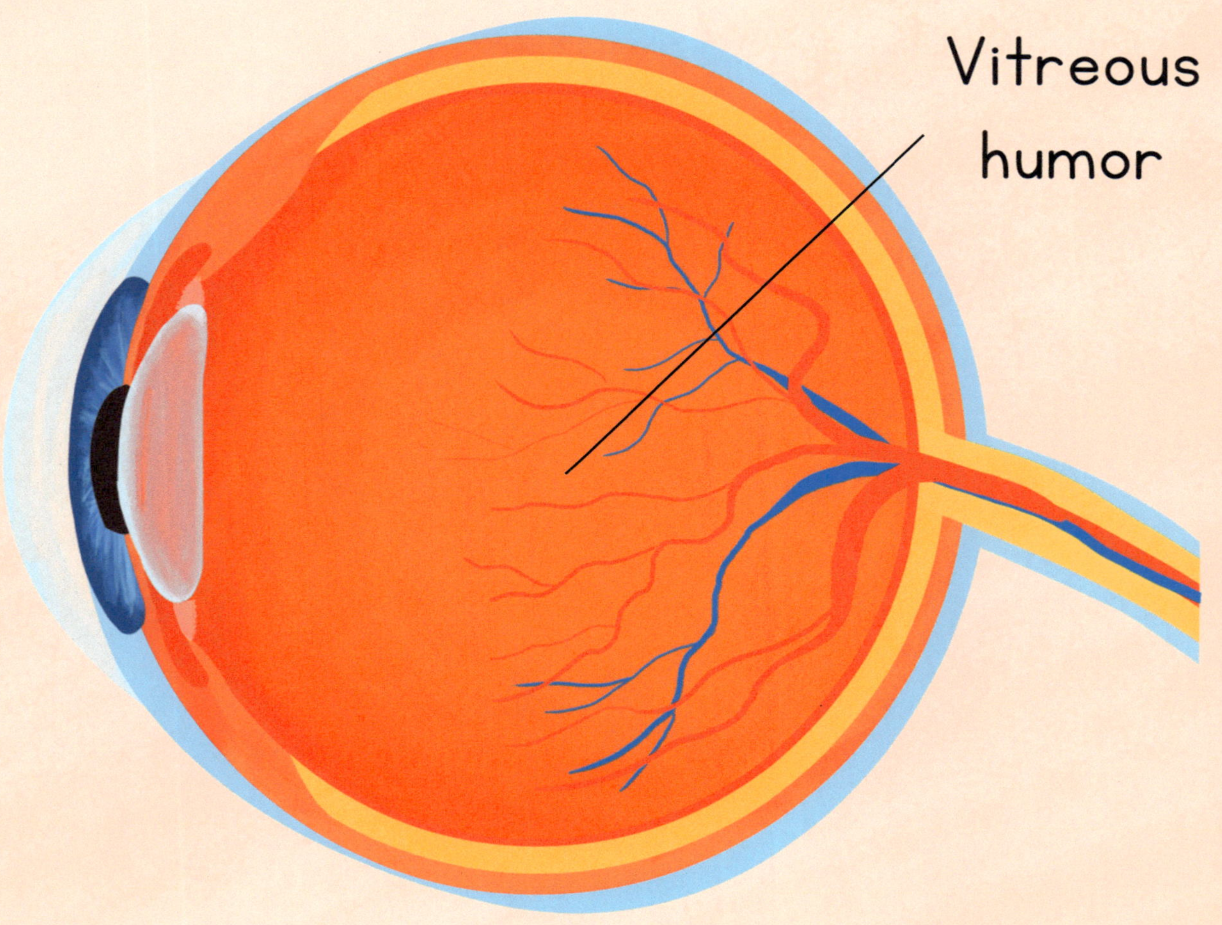

Most of the eye is filled with a clear jelly-like fluid called **vitreous humor.**

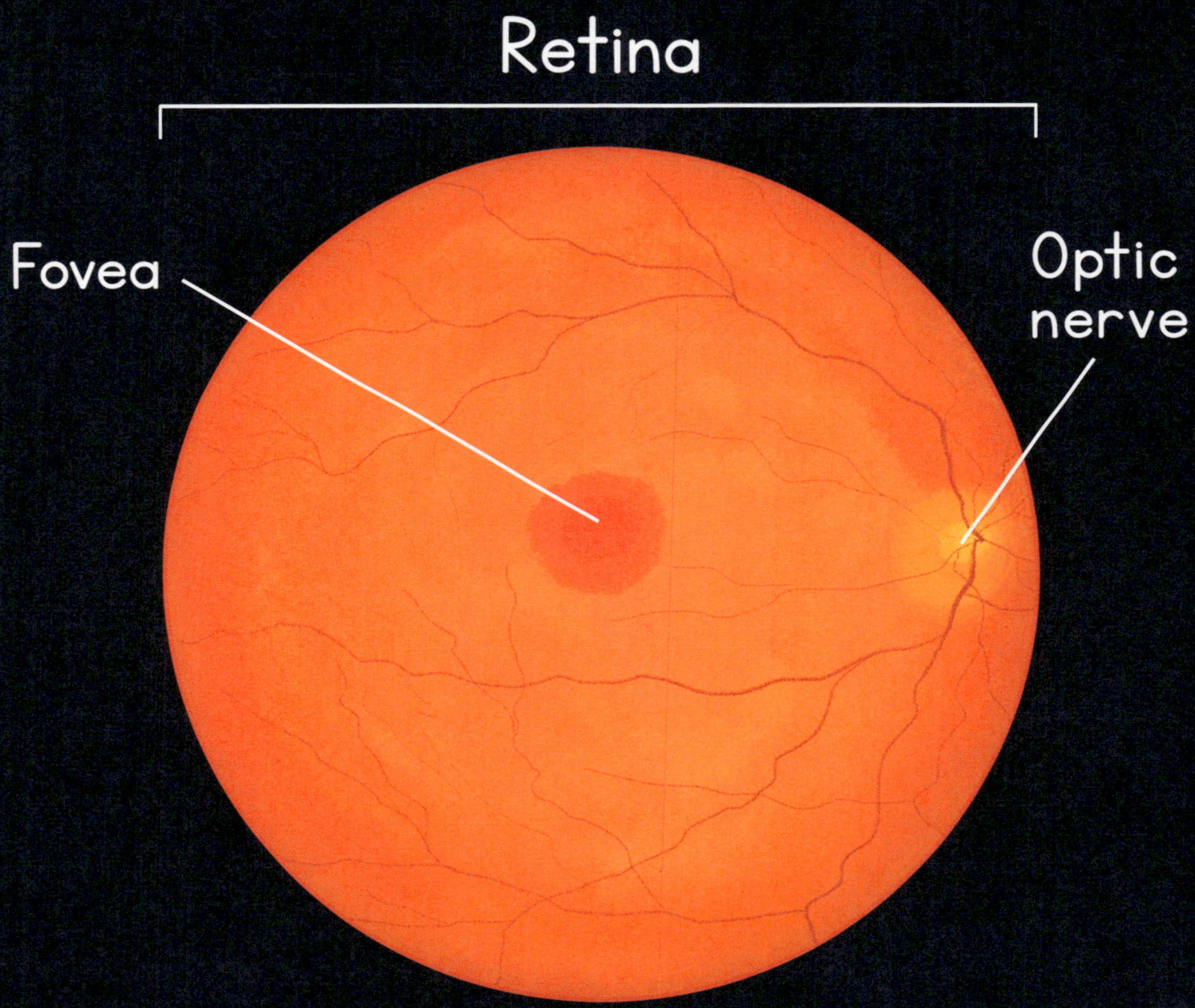

Retina

Fovea

Optic nerve

The **retina** is located in the back of the eye. It senses light and allows us to see. Near the center of the retina is the fovea.

Normal

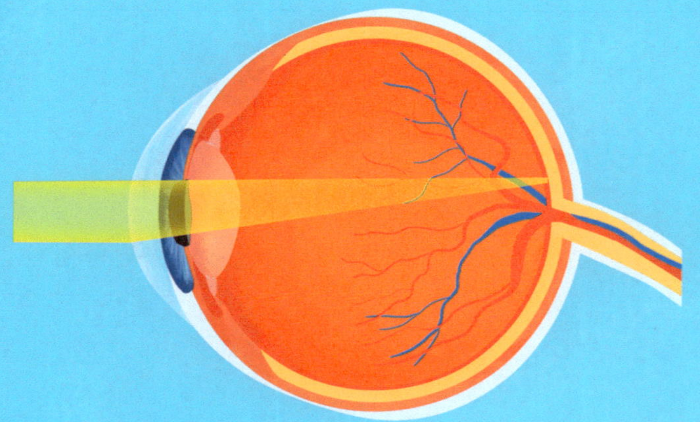

Nearsighted

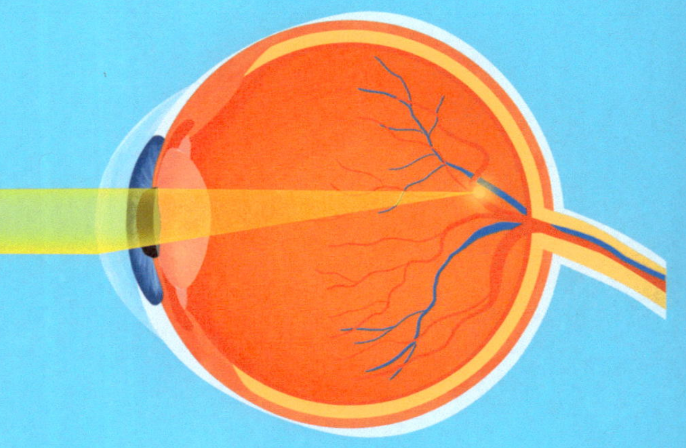

In some people, light focuses in *front* of the retina. These people are **nearsighted**, because they see best when objects are *near*.

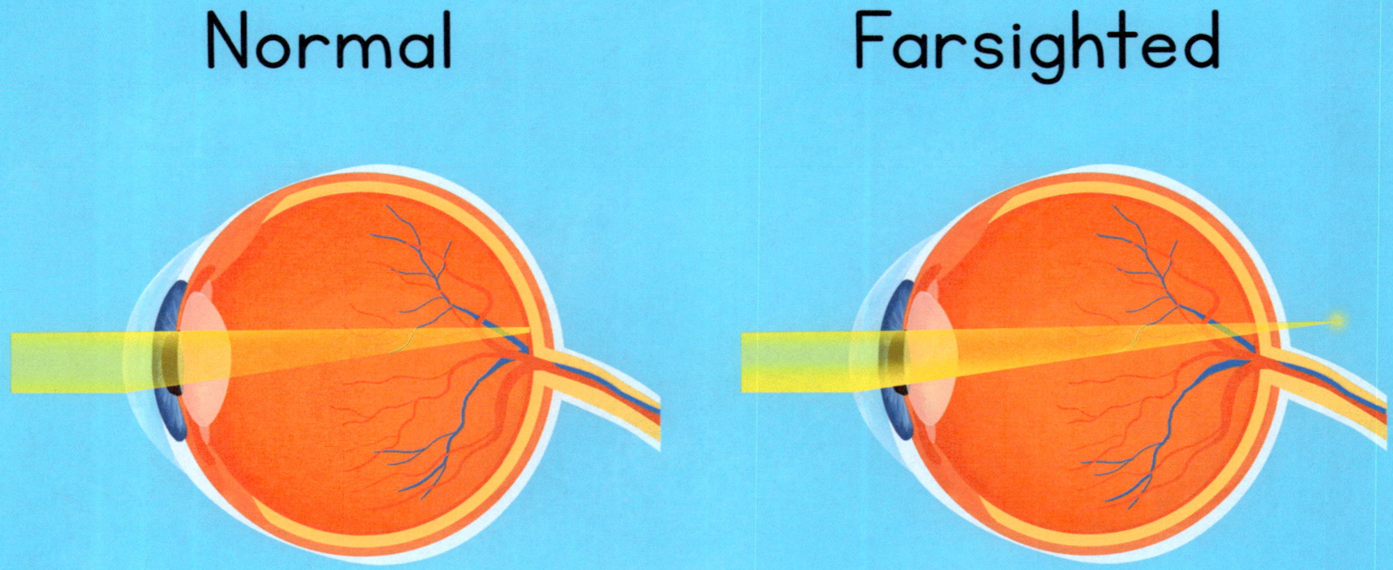

Normal

Farsighted

In other people, light focuses *behind* the retina. These people are **farsighted**, because they see best when objects are *far*.

Nearsighted and farsighted people wear glasses to see more clearly.

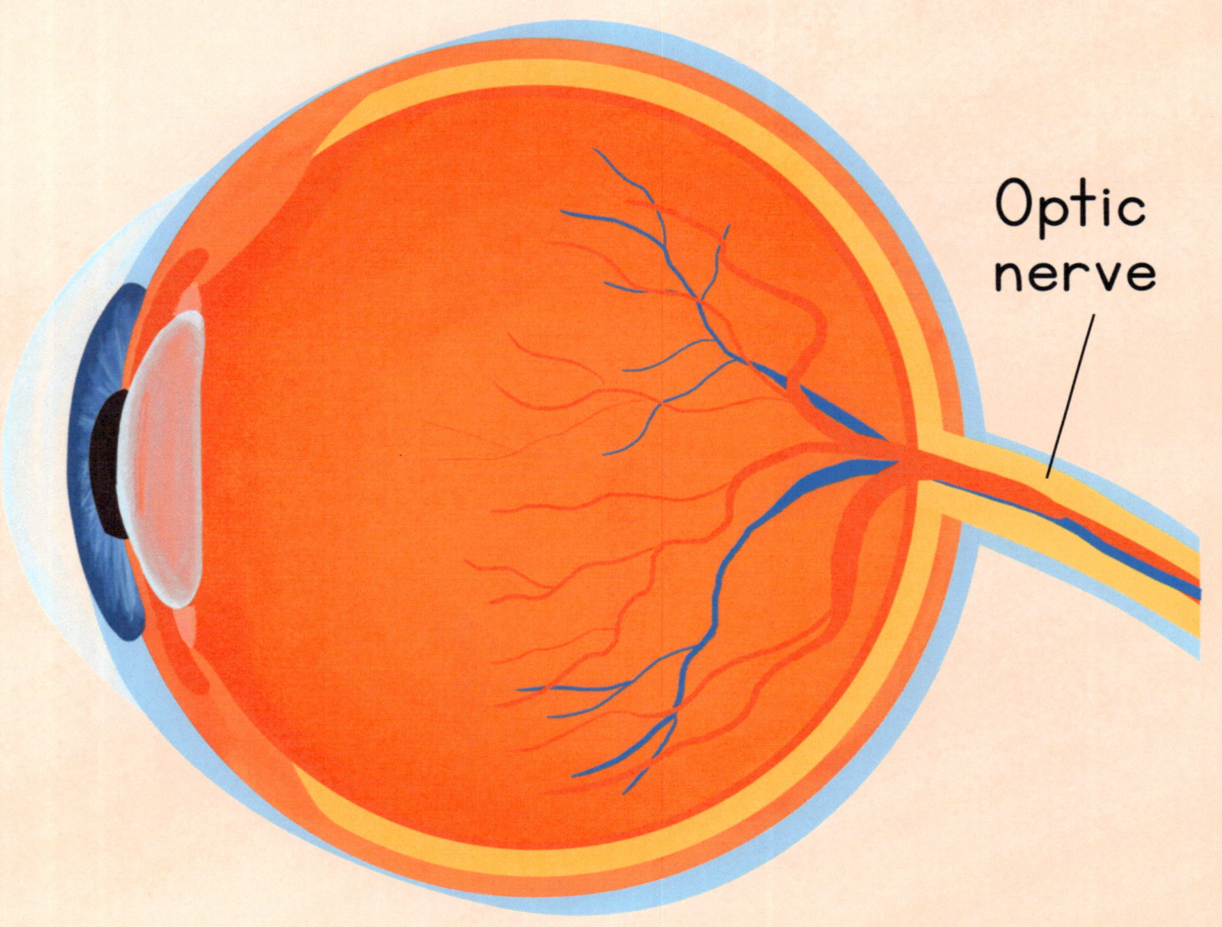

After the retina senses light, it sends this information to the brain through the **optic nerve**.

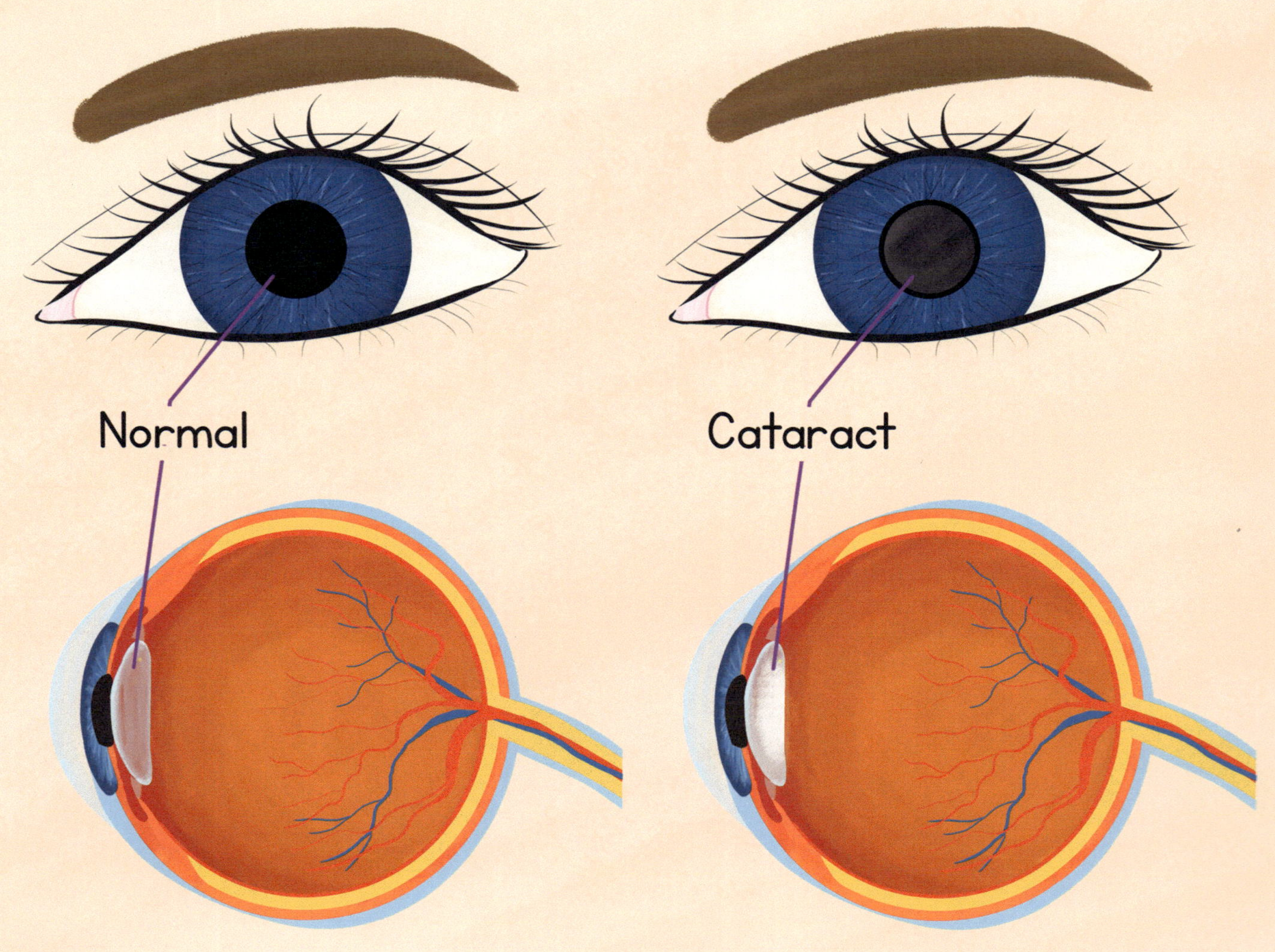

As people age, the lens can become cloudy, instead of clear. This is called a **cataract**.

People with cataracts can have trouble driving at night because of blurry vision and glare from lights on the road.

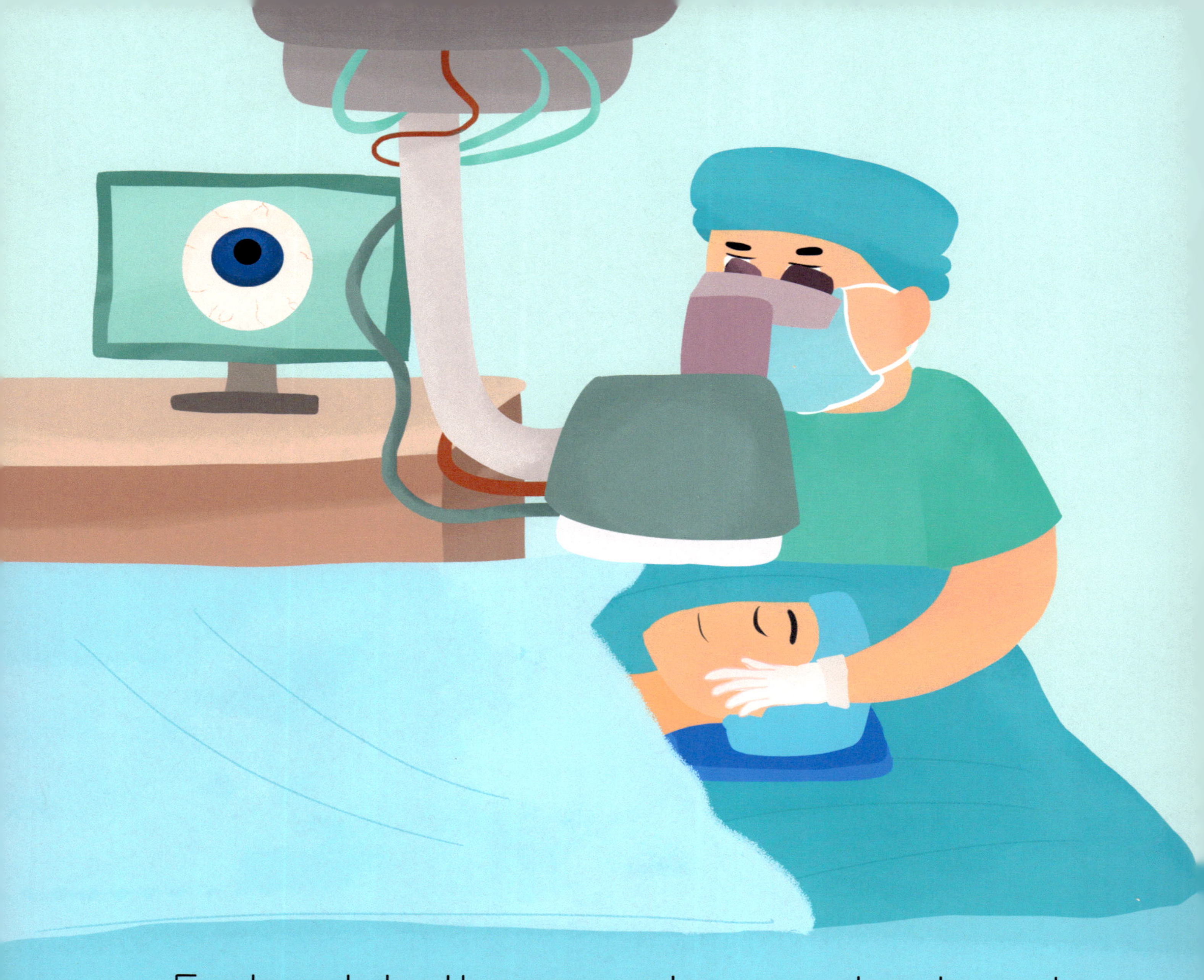

Fortunately, these people can get cataract surgery to see clearly again.

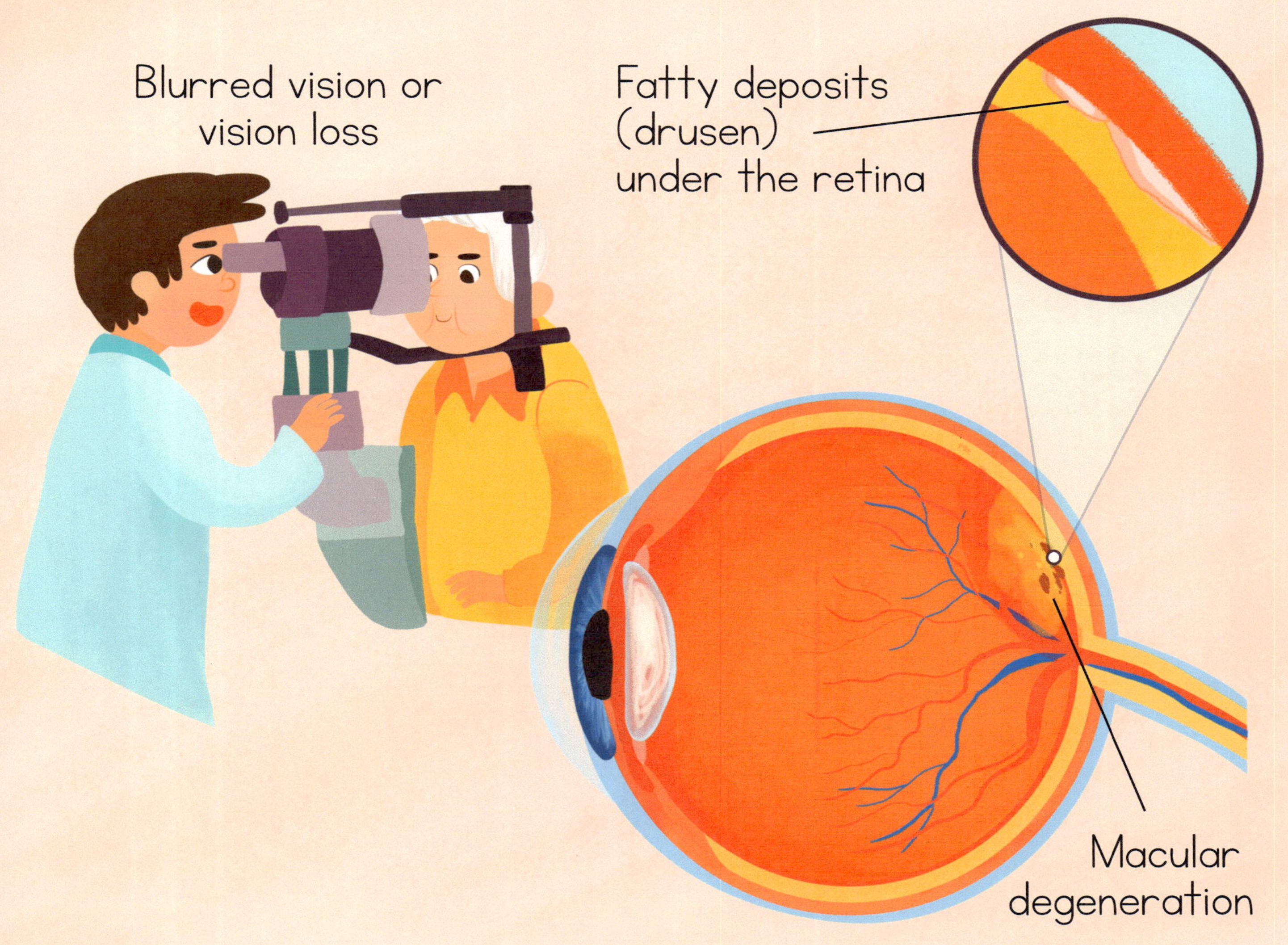

Older people can also have damage to their retina, caused by **macular degeneration**.

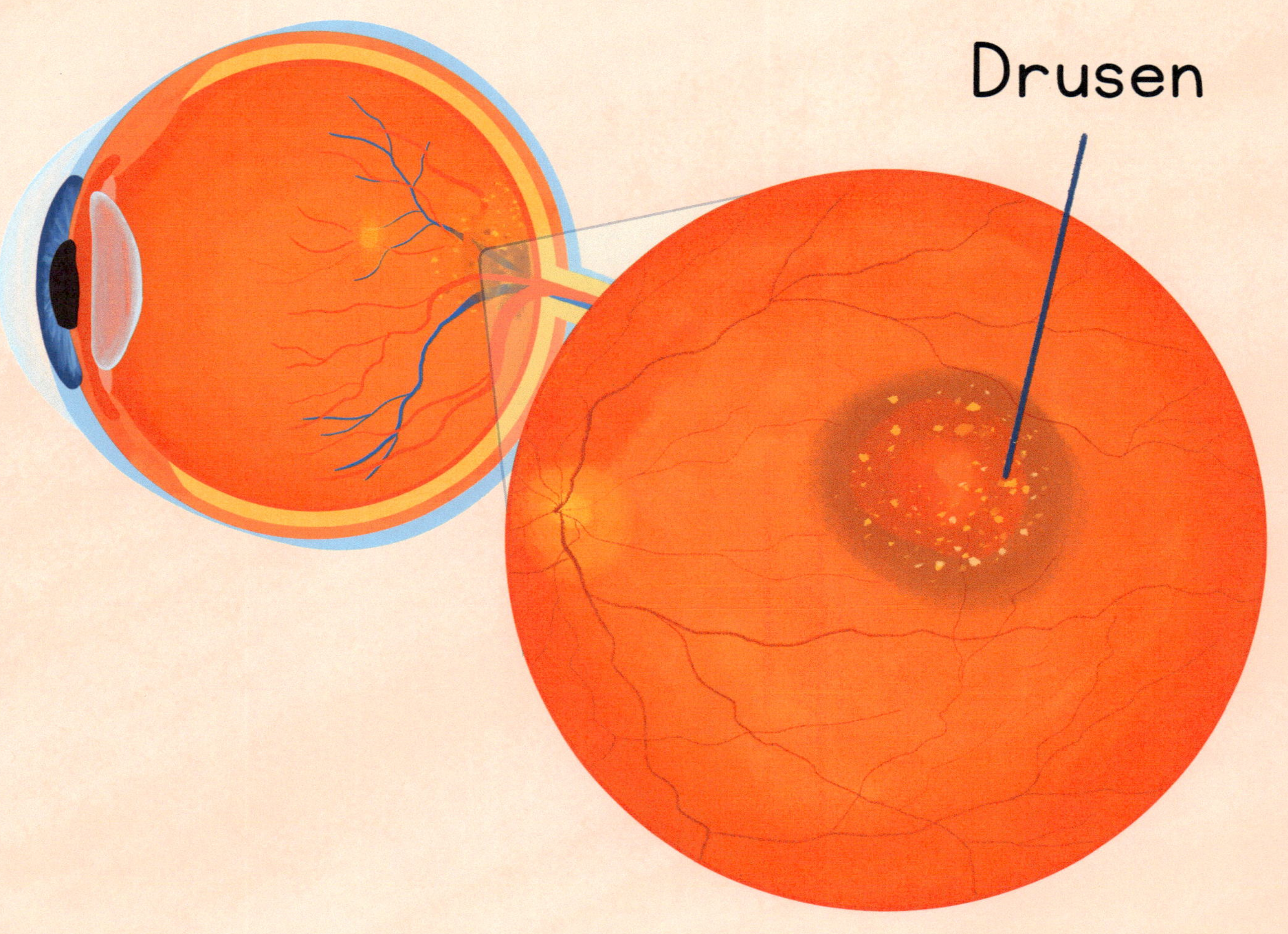

Drusen are small yellow or white spots under the retina that can be early signs of macular degeneration.

People with macular degeneration can have a black spot in the center of their vision.

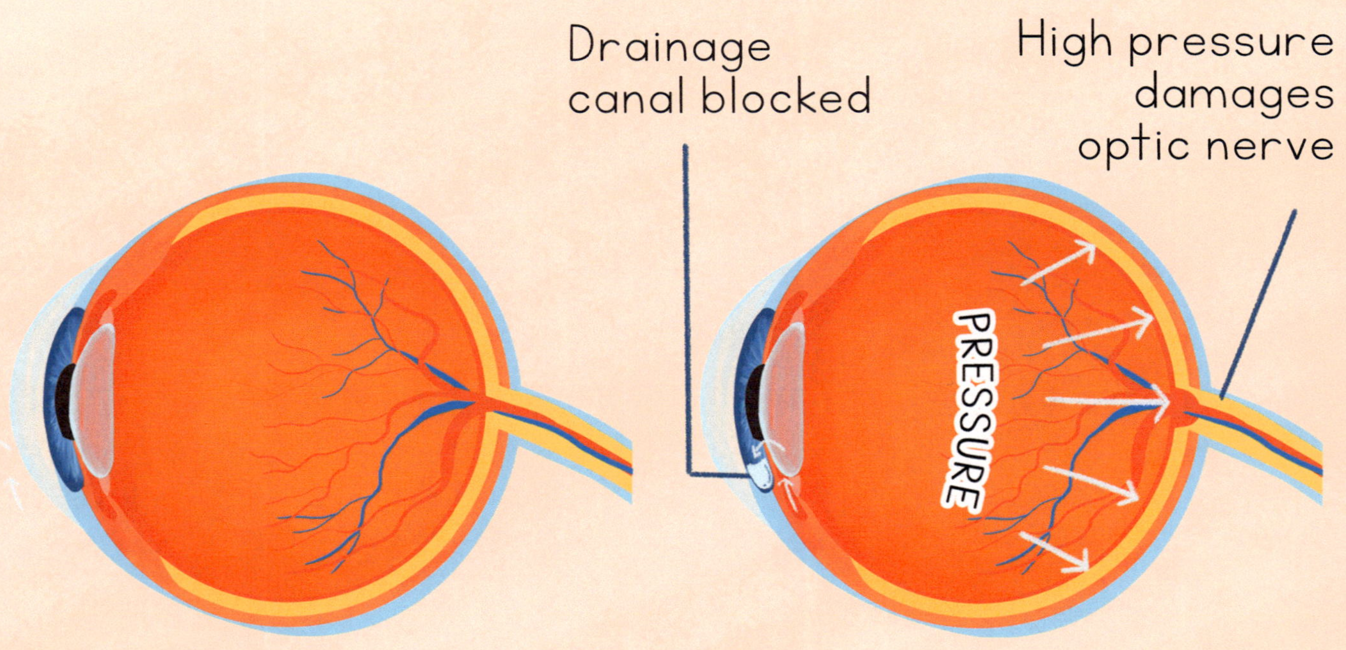

Some people can have high pressure in the eye that damages the optic nerve, a condition called **glaucoma.**

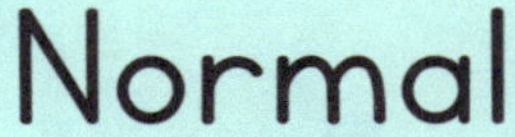

Glaucoma

Patients with glaucoma usually see normally in the center of their vision, but they can lose peripheral vision.

Fortunately, these people can take eye drops that lower pressure in the eye to help maintain vision.

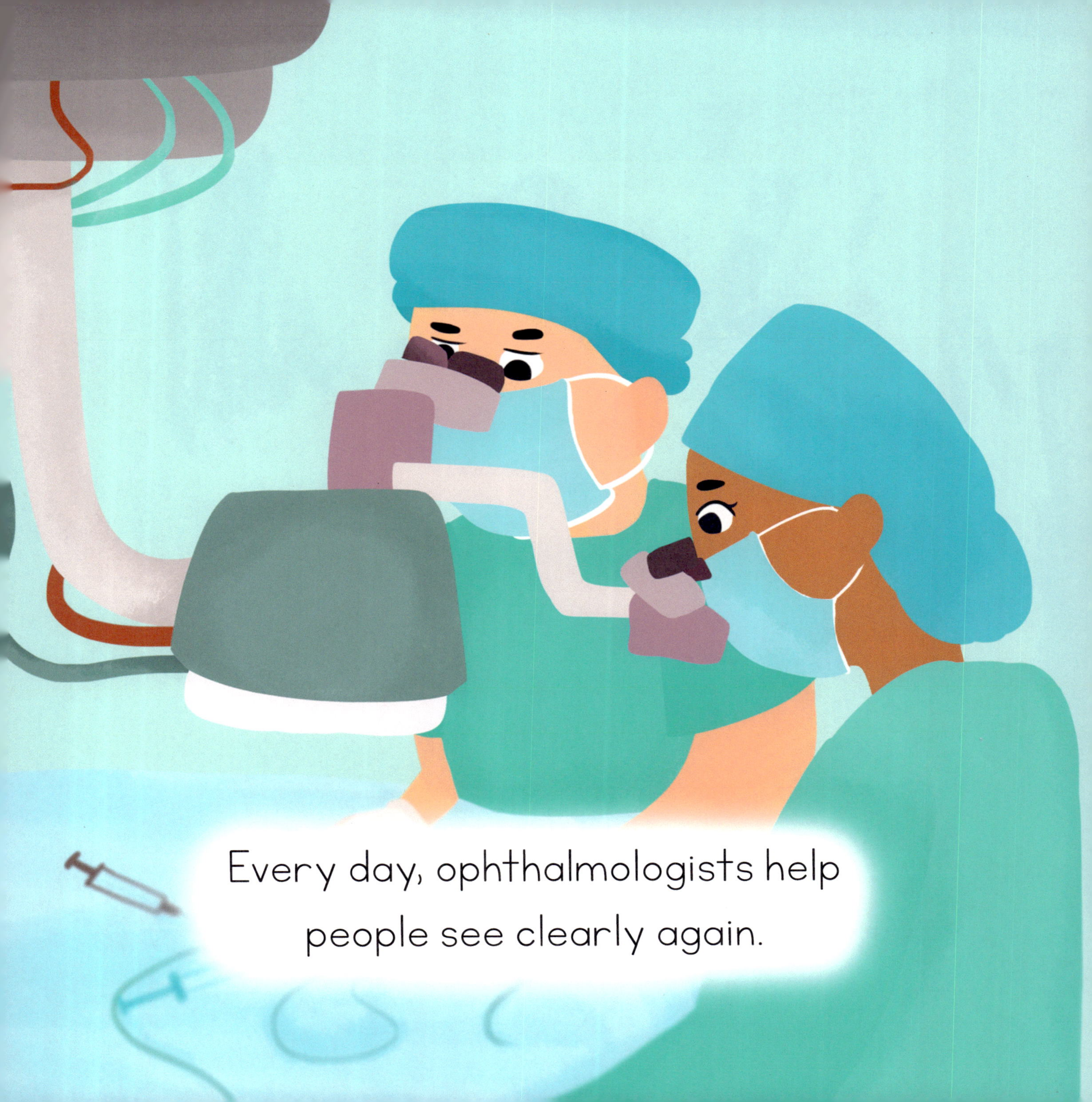

Every day, ophthalmologists help people see clearly again.

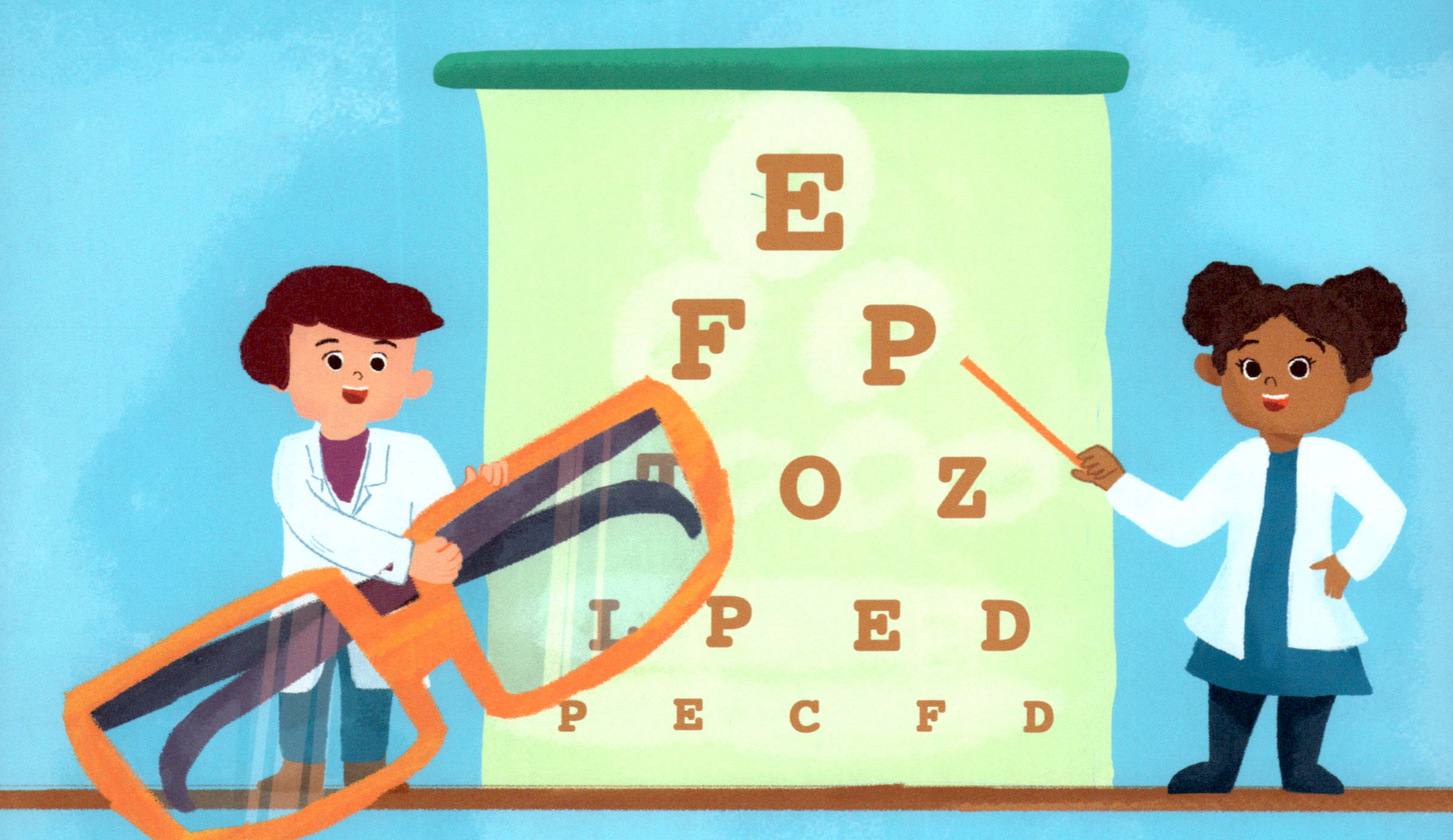

YOU'RE A FUTURE OPHTHALMOLOGIST!

Glossary

Cataract (KA-tr-akt): cloudy lens that can cause blurry vision and glare

Cornea (KOR-nee-uh): clear outer layer in the front of the eye

Drusen (DROO-sn): small yellow or white deposits under the retina that may be an early sign of macular degeneration

Farsighted: unable to clearly see objects that are close to the eye due to light rays focusing behind the retina

Glaucoma (glaa-KOW-muh): condition of increased pressure within the eye that can cause gradual peripheral vision loss

Iris (AI-ruhs): flat, colored, ring-shaped membrane behind the cornea

Lens: clear structure behind the iris that helps focus light onto the retina

Macular degeneration: degenerative condition affecting the central part of the retina (the macula) that can cause central vision loss

Nearsighted: unable to clearly see objects that are far from the eye due to light rays focusing in front of the retina

Optic nerve: cable that transmits information about what we see from the eye to the brain

Pupil (PYOO-pl): opening in the iris that allows light to enter the eye

Retina (REH-tuh-nuh): innner layer in the back of the eye that senses light

Sclera (SKLEHR-uh): white outer layer of the eye

Vitreous humor (VI-tree-uhs): clear jelly-like fluid that fills up most of the space in the eye

Let's review what you learned!

1. What is the outer clear part in the front of the eye called?
2. What is the outer white part of the eye called?.
3. What is the colored part of the eye called?
4. What is the small hole in the eye that allows light to enter the eye called?
5. What is the clear part in the eye that helps focus light called?
6. What is the jelly-like fluid in the eye called?
7. What part of the eye senses light?
8. Light that focuses in front of the retina causes ____ sightedness.
9. Light that focuses behind the retina causes ___ sightedness.
10. What is a cloudy lens that can cause blurry vision and glare called?
11. Macular degeneration is characterized by damage to what part of the eye?
12. Glaucoma is characterized by damage to what part of the eye?
13. How do eye drops prescribed to glaucoma patients affect eye pressure?
14. Does macular degeneration cause central or peripheral vision loss?
15. Does glaucoma cause central or peripheral vision loss?

Your Answers

1. ______________________
2. ______________________
3. ______________________
4. ______________________
5. ______________________
6. ______________________
7. ______________________
8. ______________________
9. ______________________
10. ______________________
11. ______________________
12. ______________________
13. ______________________
14. ______________________
15. ______________________

Answer Key

1. Cornea
2. Sclera
3. Iris
4. Pupil
5. Lens
6. Vitreous humor
7. Retina
8. Near
9. Far
10. Cataract
11. Retina (specifically the macula, which is the center of the retina)
12. Optic nerve
13. Decrease eye pressure
14. Central vision loss
15. Peripheral vision loss

About the Authors

Betty Nguyen

Betty Nguyen was born in California but spent much of her childhood in Georgia, where her parents worked on a chicken farm. She received a bachelor's degree in Biology from UCLA, where she received a full-ride Gates Millennium Scholarship through the Bill & Melinda Gates Foundation. Betty also received a full-tuition scholarship to attend medical school at the University of California, Riverside. Outside of work, Betty is a certified yoga instructor and licensed scuba diver. She also enjoys journalistic writing, cycling, and walking her two dogs in her free time.

Brandon Pham

Brandon Pham was born and raised in California. He received a bachelor's degree in Microbiology, Immunology, and Molecular Genetics from UCLA, where he was a national Goldwater Scholar. He graduated from Stanford Medical School and is currently completing his residency in ophthalmology at the Bascom Palmer Eye Institute in Miami, Florida. Brandon spent many years teaching for several national test-preparation companies and is passionate about medical education for students of all ages. In his free time, Brandon enjoys traveling, playing tennis, and distance running.

Check out the rest of the books in our series!

www.mdforkids.org

Made in the USA
Columbia, SC
23 March 2024